RUNNYMEDE R

‘Education For All’

A summary of the Swann report on the education of ethnic minority children

The Runnymede Trust

Published by the Runnymede Trust 1985
37A Grays Inn Road, London WC1X 8PP
ISBN 0 902397 55 9

Designed by Hilary Arnott
Typeset by Nancy White
Printed by Trojan Printing Co-operative

Preface

This short pamphlet provides a summary of the report, *Education for All: the report of the Committee of Inquiry into the Education of Children from Ethnic Minority Groups*, more commonly known as the Swann report, after its chairman, Lord Swann.

The Committee was established in 1979 under the chairmanship of Anthony Rampton, with the following terms of reference:

> Recognising the contribution of schools in preparing all pupils for life in a society which is both multi-racial and culturally diverse, the Committee is required to: review in relation to schools the educational needs and attainments of children from ethnic minority groups taking account, as necessary, of factors outside the formal education system relevant to school performance, including influences in early childhood and prospects for school leavers; consider the potential value of instituting arrangements for keeping under review the educational performance of different ethnic minority groups, and what those arrangements might be; consider the most effective use of resources for these purposes; and to make recommendations.

An interim report, *West Indian Children in Our Schools*, was published in June 1981 (Cmnd 8273, HMSO). In the same year, Lord Swann replaced Anthony Rampton as chairman. The Committee's final report was published in March 1985 (Cmnd 9453, HMSO).

As far as has been possible, this summary uses the language of the report itself and includes no editorial comments. It should be emphasised, however, that this summary is quite 'unofficial' and neither the Swann Committee, nor any of its individual members, have been involved in its preparation. The choice of what to put in (and to leave out) and of emphasis is that of the publishers.

We would like to thank the Hilden Charitable Fund for financial assistance with the publication of this pamphlet.

Contents

1. The nature of society

A multi-racial society such as ours would function most effectively and harmoniously on the basis of pluralism which enables, expects and encourages members of all ethnic groups, minority and majority, to participate fully in shaping the society as a whole within the framework of commonly accepted values, practices and procedures, whilst also allowing and, where necessary, assisting the ethnic minority communities in maintaining their distinct ethnic identities within this common framework. In a democratic pluralist society, all members of that society, regardless of ethnic origin, have an obligation to abide by the laws of the country and to seek to change them only through peaceful and democratic means, but there is also an obligation on government to ensure equal treatment and protection by the law for members of all groups, together with equality of access to education and employment, equal freedom and opportunity to participate fully in social and political life, equal freedom of cultural expression and equal freedom of conscience.

The ethnic majority community in a truly pluralist society cannot expect to remain untouched and unchanged by the presence of ethnic minority groups – indeed the concept of pluralism implies seeing the very diversity of such a society as an enrichment of the experience of all those within it. Similarly, the ethnic minority communities cannot, in practice, preserve all elements of their cultures and lifestyles unchanged in their entirety – indeed if they were to wish to do so it would in many cases be impossible for them to take on the shared values of the wider pluralist society. They must nevertheless be free within the democratic framework to maintain those elements which they themselves consider to be the most essential to their sense of ethnic identity. A democratic pluralist society seeks to achieve a balance between, on the one hand, the maintenance and active support of the essential elements of the cultures and lifestyles of all the ethnic groups within it, and, on the other, the acceptance by all groups of a set of shared values distinctive of the society as a whole.

This pluralist ideal is far from being realised. Many within the majority community appear to be largely oblivious to the significance of the multi-racial nature of society and where the minority communities are accepted as belonging here it frequently seems to be very much on the understanding that there is an onus on them to adapt their lifestyles to conform to the traditional British way of life so as to cause as little disruption as possible to the lives of the majority community. Unless major efforts are made to reconcile the concerns and aspirations of both the majority and minority communities along more genuinely pluralist lines, there is a real risk of the fragmentation of our society along ethnic lines which would seriously threaten the stability and cohesion of society as a whole.

It is essential to acknowledge the reality of the multi-racial context in which we all now live, to recognise the positive benefits and opportunities which this offers, and to seek to build a society which both values the diversity within it whilst united by the cohesive force of the common aims, attributes and values. In principle, Britain can be seen as already pluralist in respects other than ethnically, for example in terms of the regional variations and various cultural groupings which are readily accepted as part of the overall British 'way of life'. What is sought is not a radically different social structure, but rather an extension of this already existing pluralism to embrace ethnic minority communities. Some people, when faced with this aim of a more genuinely pluralist society, may challenge this as in some way seeking to undermine an ill-defined and nebulous concept of 'true Britishness'. The identity of British society, however, represents an amalgam of all the various forces which have been and indeed still are at work within it and the many influences which have impinged upon it from outside. To seek to represent 'being British' as something long established and immutable fails to acknowledge that the concept is in fact dynamic and ever changing, adapting and absorbing new ideas and influences.

What is looked for is not the assimilation of the minority communities within an unchanged dominant way of life, but the 'assimilation' of *all* groups within a redefined concept of what it means to live in British society today. What is sought is not to fit ethnic minorities into a mould originally cast for a society relatively homogeneous in language, religion and culture, nor to break this mould completely and replace it with one which is in all senses 'foreign' to our established way of life. Instead, the mould should be recast in a form which retains the fundamental principles of the original but within a broader pluralist conspectus – diversity within unity.

2. Racism: theory and practice

The concept of prejudice – a preconceived opinion or bias for or against someone or something – is a fact of life in this society. Whereas people's straightforward preferences are generally open to reason and thus to change, if these attitudes have become hardened and more deeply ingrained as 'prejudices' they can be seen as no longer open to question or discussion and thus as rigid, immutable and irreversible. Because prejudice in its nature overlooks the actual qualities or merits of an individual person, it is often directed against groups of people who are assumed to share common attributes and behaviour patterns. Prejudice thus requires that one has formed a stereotype of a particular group which then allows one to judge a member according to an established set of expectations. There seem thus to be two factors which are essential for prejudices initially to be formed and subsequently maintained and even reinforced – firstly, ignorance, in the literal sense of lack of knowledge on which to base informed opinions and judgments, and, secondly, the existence and promulgation of stereotypes of particular groups of people as conveyed by the major informers of public opinion, most notably the media and the education process.

The role of education in relation to prejudice is clear – to equip a pupil with knowledge and understanding in place of ignorance and to develop his or her ability to formulate views and attitudes and to assess and judge situations on the basis of this knowledge. Education should seek to counter any mistaken impressions or inaccurate, hearsay evidence which he or she may have acquired within the family, peer group or, more broadly, from the local community or the media. It is however essential that under no circumstances does education become simply a process of indoctrinating a pupil into one particular way of thinking as the only 'right and proper' view. It is no more desirable or defensible for the education system to seek to create or perpetuate positive prejudices in favour of a particular group than to countenance negative views.

It is perhaps inevitable that ethnic minority groups, who are relative newcomers to this country, should find themselves subject to possibly the most insidious and pernicious negative form of prejudice in our society – racism. Although ethnic minority groups are an integral part of this society and indeed almost all the ethnic minority children in this country are now British-born, from the continual references to ethnic minorities as 'immigrants' and 'foreigners', this seems to be far from generally accepted by the majority community.

It is important to bear in mind that the arrival of sizeable and visible ethnic minority communities coincided with the decline of long-established traditional industries and the consequent rising unemployment. In the absence of an effective explanation of the background to these developments both in schools and in the media, this coincidence was all too readily seen as 'cause and effect' and the 'newcomers' simply blamed, quite unjustly, for the effects of the recession. In these circumstances, growing competition for housing and jobs has created particular tensions which have undoubtedly exacerbated negative prejudices against ethnic minorities.

An equally influential factor in the growth of racial prejudice has been the general lack of knowledge amongst the ethnic majority community of ethnic minority communities which in turn has allowed inaccurate stereotypes to flourish. The most immediately relevant to education are clearly those which relate to the expectations which the education system appears to have of ethnic minority pupils, such as 'West Indian children will be good at sports, but "not academic" '. Some of the stereotypes of ethnic minorities can be seen as a legacy of history – from the days of the British Empire – and as a consequence of the view of other nations and peoples as in some sense 'inferior', which was until recently promulgated through the curriculum offered by many schools.

Much of the responsibility for the creation and continuance of stereotypes of ethnic minority youngsters within the education system can be seen to derive from inadequate or even misleading attempts to explain the background of ethnic minorities which may in fact serve to resurrect and perpetuate inaccurate stereotypes. In discussing stereotypes it is impossible not to take account of the pervasive influence of all branches of the media. A report by a group of teachers emphasised the generally negative way in which ethnic minority groups were treated in a range of TV programmes and concluded that such treatment tended to reinforce stereotypes or link members of ethnic minority groups to a problem. The education system can and must play a major part in challenging the stereotyping of ethnic minority communities in order to counter the pervasive influence of racism.

Comparatively little research has been carried out on teachers' attitudes towards ethnic minority pupils or on the extent to which a teacher's expectations of a pupil can directly affect that pupil's achievement or behaviour. The broad consensus of the findings of the studies reviewed by the National Foundation for Educational Research was that some teachers did have clear stereotypes of the West Indian pupil and the Asian pupil, that these stereotypes were quite different – that of the former being generally negative and that of the latter generally positive – and that the stereotypes of West Indian pupils tended to be more uniform, more firmly established and more strongly held.

While in the wider society racism may be either overt and intentional or covert and unintentional, in the educational context it is the latter which gives cause for greatest concern. The particular expectations and attitudes held by many teachers, not only of West Indian pupils but of pupils from the whole range of ethnic minority groups, have a major role in the educational experience and perhaps the academic achievements of these pupils. If teachers allow themselves to be influenced by, and even to perpetuate, stereotypes of ethnic groups, their ability to educate a pupil from a particular group may, however unwittingly, be undermined and it can become all too easy to ascribe the pupil's behaviour or performance to the assumed stereotype rather than to exercise professional judgment.

The attitude of 'colour blindness', which makes no distinction between black and white pupils, is a very widespread one among teachers and it is clear that there is a substantial body of opinion within the teaching profession which firmly believes that to recognise differences between people of various ethnic origins is divisive and can in fact constitute an obstacle to creating a harmonious multi-racial society. 'Colour blindness', however, is as potentially negative as a straightforward rejection of people with a different skin colour since both types of attitude seek to deny the validity of an important aspect of a person's identity.

The term 'institutional racism' is used by different people to cover a range of circumstances, and discussion of the extent of its influence and indeed even its existence is often both confused and confusing. Institutional racism describes the way in which a range of long established systems, practices and procedures, within both education and the wider society, which were originally devised to meet the needs and aspirations of a relatively homogeneous society, can now be seen not only to fail to take account of the multi-racial nature of Britain today, but may also ignore or even actively work against the interests of ethnic minority communities. Such practices include many which, whilst clearly originally well-intentioned and in no way racist in intent, can now be seen as racist in effect, in depriving members of ethnic minority groups of equality of access to the full range of opportunities which the majority community can take for granted. Institutional racism is just as much a cause for concern as the prejudiced attitudes which some individuals may hold since the establishment, in this way, of racism within the 'system' itself can serve to reinforce, to magnify and to perpetuate such attitudes, even where such attitudes are open to change. Institutional change and changing individual attitudes are of equal importance and have complementary roles to play in achieving the overall shift in emphasis and outlook which are essential in relation to today's multi-racial society.

In considering the influence which racism, whether intentional or unintentional, can have on the education process, it is essential to recognise the very direct and acute bearing which the general 'climate' of racism in this country has on what takes place in the school classroom. By this is meant the way in which the confidence of ethnic minorities to see themselves as an integral part of our society and thus as having equal claim to shaping their own futures within it, has been undermined and to some extent lost entirely. The extent of racial disadvantage has been well-documented, while two other aspects of the pressure felt by ethnic minorities and raised repeatedly by parents and young people, and which have undoubtedly contributed greatly to the overall climate of racism, are the fear of racial harassment and attack, and the uncertainty created by the policies of successive governments on immigration and nationality.

If in the face of forms of racism such as racial harassment, or indeed in the face of ignorant and inaccurate statements about ethnic minorities, the school seeks simply to remain neutral and uninvolved, this is a failure, not only in terms of educational responsibilities but also in effect condoning and encouraging the persistence of such occurrences. It is difficult for ethnic minority communities to have full confidence and trust in an institution which they see as simply ignoring or dismissing what is in fact an ever present and all pervasive shadow over their everyday lives.

Racism is an insidious evil which, for the sake of the future unity and stability of society, must be countered. A clear distinction can be drawn between what can be seen as 'individual' racism and the broader and more pervasive 'climate' of racism and, within that, the way institutions and established practices and procedures may serve to reinforce, perpetuate and extend this.

Racism in all these forms, however, needs to be tackled in the interests of the community as a whole, since it damages not only the groups seen and treated as in some way inferior or manipulable, but also the more powerful groups in that it feeds them with a totally false sense of superiority and this distorts their understanding of themselves and the world around them. All members of a racist society suffer from feelings of fear and insecurity, and it takes little to fan the flames of suspicion and mistrust into open hatred and violence.

For schools to allow racist attitudes to persist unchecked in fact constitutes a fundamental mis-education for their pupils. Schools may not be able to lead change directly but they should be capable of leading to change by creating an overall unity of purpose which will encompass the concept that to be British you do not have to have white skin nor to have family origins only in this country.

3. Achievement and underachievement

West Indian children on average are underachieving at school. By contrast, Asian children show on average a pattern of achievement which resembles that of white children, although there is some evidence of variation between different subgroups. In particular, Bangladeshis are seriously underachieving. Of the smaller ethnic groups, some are underachieving and some are not. Averages, of course, conceal much variation. There are West Indian children who do well, as well as Asian children who are underachieving. Possible causes for the differences in *average* achievement between Asian and West Indian children include the tightly knit nature of the Asian family and community – since parental and family influences on educational success in general have long been recognised this seems to be a factor to be borne in mind. In addition, the differences may be explained in that Asians are given to 'keeping their heads down' and adopting a 'low profile', thereby making it easier to succeed in a hostile environment, whereas West Indians are given to protest, with the reverse effect. Given the different histories of the two groups, this is not an improbable explanation, but it is a stereotype judgment and, as such, must be viewed with caution.

Low average IQ has often been suggested as a cause of underachievement, particularly in the case of West Indians, and this has long been disputed. Investigations show, however, that IQ is not a significant factor in underachievement.

School performance has long been shown to show a close correlation with socio-economic status and social class. Ethnic minorities are particularly disadvantaged in social and economic terms, and there can no longer be any doubt that this extra deprivation is the result of racial prejudice and discrimination, especially in the areas of employment and housing. This extra deprivation, over and above that of disadvantaged whites, leads in many instances to an *extra* element of underachievement. A substantial part of ethnic minority underachievement is thus the result of racial prejudice and discrimination on the part of society at large, bearing on ethnic minority homes and families, and hence, indirectly, on children. Nevertheless, it would be quite wrong to assume that low socio-economic status must lead inevitably to low attainment and any teacher who expected low achievement would be failing in his or her task as an educator.

Not all underachievement is to be accounted for in these terms and the rest is due in large measure to prejudice and discrimination bearing directly on children, within the educational system, as well as outside it. The findings of the research evidence about racial prejudice and discrimination in the educational system are, however, inconclusive when it comes to deciding which factors may be important. The issues involved are complex and ill-understood and much more research is needed to understand the problems.

It will be evident that society is faced with a dual problem: eradicating the discriminatory attitudes of the white majority on the one hand, and on the other, evolving an educational system which ensures that *all* pupils reach their full potential. In the short term, the first of these problems is a matter for the law, the government, housing authorities, employers, unions, the Commission for Racial Equality and others. But in the long term, it is for schools to bring about the much-needed change in attitudes amongst coming generations. The second problem is specifically one for the educational system. A start has been made in recent years, but there is still a long way to go before schools bring out the full potential of all their pupils, and in this context, particularly their ethnic minority pupils.

This dual approach to one of Britain's most serious social concerns leads to the concept of 'Education for All' – an attempt simultaneously to change attitudes amongst the white majority, and to develop a pattern of education that enables all pupils to give of their best.

4. 'Education for All': a new approach

The absence of clear policy objectives based on firm educational principles, rather than determined by political expediency, from the early days of large-scale immigration has led to the development of piecemeal and *ad hoc* measures around the country, varying from those multi-racial schools and areas which are now, in theory at least, committed to their interpretation of 'multicultural education', to others which have ignored or rejected the need for any initiatives in the belief that any problems which may exist will solve themselves given time – a truly 'laissez faire' philosophy. At the same time, areas of the country which as yet have little or no ethnic minority settlement appear to have remained oblivious to the changed and changing nature of British society and convinced that this has no relevance to the education of their pupils.

Much of the confusion which exists in the multicultural field derives from the fact that there are two distinct dimensions to the debate. On the one hand, meeting the educational needs of ethnic minority pupils and, on the other, broadening the education offered to all pupils to reflect the multi-racial nature of British society. Whilst these two issues are clearly interrelated and complementary, it is now possible and indeed essential to see them within a new and broader perspective – that of offering all pupils a good, relevant and up to date education for life in Britain and the world as it is today.

It could be suggested that, within Britain's decentralised education system, it is neither appropriate nor desirable to seek to dictate policy too closely to LEAs or schools. Such a view assumes, however, that an appropriate educational response to the multi-racial nature of society will simply 'emerge' without any assistance or direction from the centre. A review of developments in this field over recent years shows clearly that, far from a consensus emerging of what needs to be done, there seems to have been a marked divergence of view as LEAs and schools have continued to develop their own 'brands' of multicultural education, with little reference to activities in other areas of the country. As long as the underlying climate of racism is allowed to persist unchallenged, it seems likely that, as one staff working party put it, 'Multicultural education will not just happen, rather natural prejudice and institutionalised discrimination will dominate'.

It is essential to change fundamentally the terms of the debate about the educational response to today's multi-racial society and to look ahead to educating all children, from whatever ethnic group, to an understanding of the shared values of society as a whole as well as to an appreciation of the diversity of lifestyles and cultural, linguistic and religious backgrounds which make up this society and the wider world. In so doing, all pupils should be given the owledge and skills needed, not only to contribute positively to shaping the future nature of British society, but also to determine their own individual identities.

The term 'multicultural education' appears to have encouraged schools and LEAs in 'all-white' areas to believe that the issues involved are of no concern to them since they see themselves as mono-cultural, and the term seems therefore to have added to the confusion which already exists about the aims and objectives involved. The simple phrase 'Education for All' describes more accurately the desired approach to education since it reflects the responsibility shared by all those concerned with education in laying the foundations for the pluralist society already described.

The concept of 'Education for All'

The essential steps in the argument for 'Education for All' are as follows:

- the fundamental change that is necessary is the recognition that the problem facing the education system is not how to educate children of ethnic minorities, but how to educate *all* children;
- Britain is a multi-racial and multicultural society and all pupils must be enabled to understand what this means;
- this challenge cannot be left to the separate and independent initiatives of LEAs and schools: only those with experience of substantial numbers of ethnic minority pupils have attempted to tackle it, though the issue affects all schools and all pupils;
- education has to be something more than the reinforcement of the beliefs, values and identity which each child brings to school;
- it is necessary to combat racism, to attack inherited myths and stereotypes, and the ways in which they are embodied in institutional practices;
- multicultural understanding has to permeate all aspects of a school's work; it is not a separate topic that can be welded on to existing practices;
- only in this way can schools begin to offer anything approaching the equality of opportunity for all pupils which it must be the aspiration of the education system to provide.

The strategy for implementation of 'Education for All' requires that:

- the response of schools, both multi-racial and 'all-white', to cultural diversity has to be seen as a central feature of the current debate on the balance and breadth of the school curriculum and the Secretary of State should focus on this issue in considering the responses to DES Circular 8/83 on the curriculum and in any further statements that he may make and any agreements that he may seek about the curriculum;
- all LEAs should declare their commitment to the principles of 'Education for All', to the development of a pluralist approach to the curriculum and to countering the influence of racism;
- every LEA should have at least one adviser and perhaps a senior officer with responsibility to promote the policies put forward here, to act as a catalyst to

encourage teachers and other advisers to reflect a pluralist perspective in their work;

- HM Inspectorate should give attention to the extent to which the curriculum takes full account of the multi-racial nature of society and should highlight, in their reports, including reports on individual schools, instances of 'good practice' and areas of concern;
- HM Inspectorate should issue clear guidance on the practical implications of adopting a pluralist approach to the curriculum and on ways of countering the influence of racism on schools;
- the School Curriculum Development Committee should establish a series of subject working parties to consider how areas of the curriculum can be made to reflect more fully the diversity of British society, and to offer guidance;
- the School Curriculum Development Committee should review existing materials which reflect a pluralist approach to the curriculum. The Committee should consider how these materials may be made more widely known and how the production of further such resources may be stimulated;
- examining boards should reflect cultural diversity in the syllabuses they offer and in their working practices;
- the Secondary Examinations Council should cooperate with the School Curriculum Development Committee to ensure that initiatives to broaden the school curriculum are reflected by parallel developments within the examination system;
- all LEAs should expect their schools to produce clear policy statements on 'Education for All' and monitor their practical implementation;
- all schools, whether multi-racial or 'all-white', should review their work in the light of the principles put forward; in secondary schools it may be necessary to establish departmental working parties to appraise provision in different subject areas;
- all schools should adopt clear policies to combat racism;
- the government should provide every maintained school in the country with a summary of this report;
- the DES should orqanise a series of reqional conferences for elected members of LEAs, teachers and other educationists to consider the implications of this report. The conclusions of these conferences might subsequently be drawn to the attention of a wider audience in a conference report;
- the government should revise the provisions of section 11 of the Local Government Act 1966 to make it more appropriate to the needs of the ethnic minority communities;
- the Secretary of State should include a growing number of initiatives and pilot projects designed to develop a broader, pluralist approach to the curriculum within arrangements for education support grants;
- the DES should implement the recommendations of the interim report relating to the collection of ethnically-based statistics within education.

5. Language and language education

There is now a great diversity of languages spoken amongst British families in British homes. In order to lay the foundations for a genuinely pluralist society the education system must both cater for the linguistic needs of ethnic minority pupils and also take full advantage of the opportunities offered for the education of all pupils by the linguistic diversity of British society today.

Language education in a multicultural society has often in the past been seen solely in terms of the 'problem' of teaching English to children for whom it is not a first language. The language needs of ethnic minority children should no longer be compartmentalised in this way nor seen as outside the mainstream of education. A broader approach to language teaching would be beneficial to *all* pupils, and the existence of bi- or multi-lingual communities in Britain should be seen as an opportunity for all schools to broaden the linguistic horizons of all pupils by ensuring that they acquire a real understanding of the role, range and richness of language in all its forms.

English as a second language

The means by which LEAs have sought to cater for the ESL needs of pupils have varied widely. They range from the employment of teams of peripatetic staff serving a number of schools by withdrawing pupils for specialist help, to the establishment of separate language centres catering for children of all ages either on a part-time basis – having been withdrawn from their normal schools – or on a full-time basis – before being placed in mainstream schools at all.

Whatever form it takes, however, ESL provision has been seen as 'marginal' to mainstream education and to be the responsibility of specialist teachers coping with a particular educational need. Non-specialist teachers have been led to believe that they have little or no role to play in the language development of children with ESL needs.

The use of separate language centres, although originally conceived as a form of 'positive discrimination', can in retrospect be seen as a form of institutionalised racism. While not discriminatory in intent, such centres are discriminatory in effect in that they deny the child access to the full range of educational opportunities available – in the case of full-time centres by withdrawing them totally from the mainstream school and with part-time provision by requiring them to miss a substantial part of the normal school curriculum.

ESL need should *not* be met either in language centres or separate units within schools for the following reasons:

• the limitations on the breadth of curriculum which a language centre or unit can offer and the inherent injustice of denying any pupil access to other subjects until he or she has mastered English;

• the absence in many cases of direct links between the language centre or unit and the mainstream of school life which means that work being done does not mirror that of the school and that the language needs perceived by class teachers are not necessarily met by the ESL specialist;

• the possibly negative effect on a pupil's progress in learning English or mixing primarily with children for whom English is a second language;

• the possible effects in a child's socialisation and developing maturity of being separated from his or her peers and away from the 'social reality' of the school;

• the inevitable trauma for a child of entering the English-speaking environment of the mainstream school is merely postponed and not avoided;

• mainstream teachers are discouraged from regarding ethnic minority pupils' language needs as their concern and are indeed encouraged to regard ESL work as a whole as of low status.

The needs of learners of ESL should therefore be met by provision within the mainstream school as part of a comprehensive programme of language education for *all* children. ESL provision should come to be viewed as an extension of the range of language needs for which *all* teachers in schools should, provided they are given adequate training and appropriate support, be able to cater.

For the child from a home where English is not the first language, it is clear that nursery provision can be a particularly valuable stage of the overall educational experience and can serve to ease the sometimes traumatic transition between the home and school.

Within primary and secondary schools, *all* teachers with a substantial number of pupils for whom English is a second language have a responsibility to cater for linguistic needs of these pupils and should be given appropriate support and training to discharge it. However, there will still be a need for particular language specialists on a school staff who can offer support and advice to both colleagues and pupils. Teaching skills in this area should be developed primarily through school-based training.

It is recognised that there is a long way to go before this broader concept of responsibility for language needs gains general acceptance. It will not be in the interests of second language learners to lose the specialist help of ESL teachers and be simply left to 'sink or swim' within the mainstream classroom. In view of the somewhat negative attitudes of some mainstream teachers towards ESL learners, especially the correlation of 'lack of English' with 'lack of ability', there clearly needs to be a major shift in opinion in order to accord these pupils equal opportunities. The fostering of positive attitudes towards linguistic diversity is therefore a prerequisite for making integrated ESL provision a success.

Mother tongue provision

The role of the education system in relation to the maintenance and support of the language of ethnic minority communities cannot be seen in isolation from the whole question of language education and in the context of an education which meets the needs of all pupils. The term 'mother tongue provision' can in fact encompass a range of activities:

- bi-lingual education: the use of a pupil's mother tongue as a medium of instruction alongside English so that the child may be taught for a set part of the day in, for example, Punjabi and for the rest of the time in English;
- mother tongue maintenance: the development of a pupil's fluency in his or her mother tongue as an integral part of a primary school's curriculum by timetabling a number of hours each week for teaching in the mother tongue;
- mother tongue teaching: the teaching of the languages of ethnic minority communities as part of the modern languages curriculum of secondary schools alongside established languages such as French and German.

It has been argued that mother tongue provision is an important aspect of multicultural education, and that all languages should be valued and maintained as part of our national linguistic resource. Mother tongue provision has been seen as an essential step in according ethnic minority pupils 'equality of opportunity', and it has also been argued that it is the right of all pupils to receive education in their own mother tongue.

However, the value of mother tongue provision in enhancing an ethnic minority child's educational performance has not so far been borne out by any research in the UK. Despite evidence that there is considerable support for mother tongue provision amongst ethnic minority parents, parents are primarily concerned that the educational system give their children a good command of English, and that any provision for mother tongue should in no way detract from this aim. A good command of English is in fact the basis for equality of opportunity.

The case for bi-lingual education in maintained schools is not therefore supported. Similarly, mother tongue maintenance can be best achieved within the ethnic minority communities rather than in mainstream schools, but with considerable support from and liaison with the latter. The teaching of ethnic minority languages within the modern language curriculum is, however, supported.

Bi-lingual education and mother tongue maintenance require separation of ethnic minority pupils from their peers for 'special' teaching, but the withdrawal of pupils as an identifiable group and separate provision can only increase social divisions between pupils. It also leaves the majority pupils' education impoverished and mono-lingual, and leaves unaffected the negative perceptions of the 'strangeness' of ethnic minority pupils. Linguistic barriers can only be broken down by a programme of general language awareness for *all* pupils (see below). The argument that teaching ethnic minority pupils through the medium of their mother tongue accords them equality of opportunity is not supported. On the contrary, this can only be achieved through the emphasis of giving them a good command of English.

An important role in reducing the trauma for ethnic minority pupils entering the English-speaking school environment can be played by nursery and primary schools providing a 'bi-lingual resource'. This would offer psychological and social support as well as being able to explain simple educational concepts in the child's mother tongue, but always working within the mainstream classroom situation.

If a language is truly the mother tongue of a community and is the language needed for parent/child interaction and for access to the religious and cultural heritage of the community, then it will survive and flourish regardless of the provision made for its teaching and/or usage in schools. The role of the education system is therefore to develop a comprehensive system of support for existing provision for language maintenance by the communities concerned. School premises should be available free of charge for community language classes, community language teachers should have a closer relationship with the school, and LEAs should make grants available for such classes.

In order for ethnic minority languages to become more established as part of the modern language curriculum and a realistic option for *all* pupils, ethnic minority language teachers must be demonstrably 'good at their job'. At present, due to their low status within schools, this is not so. Government is urged to ensure that potential teachers of ethnic minority languages receive the degree of training, support and recognition they are entitled to expect. There is also great need for improved teaching materials and more involvement by public examining bodies in improving the syllabus content to bring the provision for these languages in line with other subjects.

Language across the curriculum

There has been little progress in implementing the concept of language across the curriculum outlined in the Bullock Report. All teachers must be encouraged continually to review their use of language in the classroom and examinations in terms of its relevance and familiarity to ethnic minority pupils. A more structured approach to the development of this policy is necessary, with the head teacher in primary schools and possibly the deputy head in secondary schools being responsible for its overall coordination.

Language awareness and linguistic diversity

All schools should seek to foster amongst their pupils an awareness of the linguistic diversity of our society and a real understanding of the role and function of language in all its forms. In schools with mono-lingual pupil populations, distance learning techniques – such as taped and video-taped materials – and pupil or teacher exchanges with multi-lingual schools should be used to enhance pupils' appreciation of linguistic diversity. LEA advisers and HMI, through in-service courses and access to materials, should seek to broaden the expertise of English teachers. Examining boards should consider the possible need to revise or extend the English syllabuses they offer to enhance pupils' understanding of the nature of language and language forms.

The 'repertoire' approach to responding to West Indian dialects has proved the most effective and positive, and is to be recommended. The intention of this approach is not to change or replace any particular dialect but to develop a sharper awareness of, and interest in, the different language forms that the child can use. This approach builds constructively on the considerable language strengths the child brings to the classroom.

6. Religion and the role of the school: religious education and the 'separate' schools debate

The broader phenomenological approach to religious education is the only means of enhancing the understanding of all pupils of the plurality of faiths in contemporary Britain, of bringing them to an understanding of the nature of belief and the religious dimension of human existence, and of helping them to appreciate the diverse and sometimes conflicting life stances which exist, and thus enabling them to determine their own religious position. The 'confessional' approach to religious education, whether in terms of encouraging a belief in the superiority of Christianity, or as advocated by some parts of the Muslim community for the teaching of Islam in separate schools, is therefore rejected.

However, this stance in no way conflicts with the role of individual faith communities in providing religious *instruction*. Indeed community-based provision for religious instruction complements rather than conflicts with the more broadly based religious education which schools should be offering to all children.

It is becoming increasingly difficult to reconcile the phenomenological approach with certain provisions of the 1944 Education Act. Specifically the requirement for a daily act of collective worship cannot be justified given the multiplicity of beliefs and non-beliefs now present in society. While not seeking to restrict the freedom of those schools who wish to continue with this requirement, the freedom *not* to make such a provision should no longer be restricted by law.

In relation to religious education – or, in the terms of the 1944 Act, religious 'instruction' – provision should not necessarily be required by law nor set within the complex framework established in the Act.

If the provision of religious education (instruction) continues to be required by law, and if there is a likelihood that the provision made may adopt a confessional approach, based on a Christian-dominated agreed syllabus, then the right of withdrawal must be retained. If, however, religious education is broadened to follow a phenomenological approach, which seeks to 'inform' rather than to 'convert' pupils, then the legal provision for withdrawal and the requirement for agreed syllabuses are no longer required. The government, in consultation with religious and educational bodies, should look afresh at the relevant provisions of the 1944 Act, to see whether alterations are called for after an interval of 40 years.

'Separate' schools debate

Some minority communities are increasingly seeking to establish their own separate schools within the existing mainstream system, ie, voluntary aided schools. This right is firmly enshrined in law under the 1944 Education Act, and many Church of England, Roman Catholic and Jewish voluntary aided schools already exist. The overriding concern of ethnic minority groups supporting separate schools is the nature of religious education and the general 'ethos' provided by mainstream schools. There is a widespread belief that their religions are not dealt with in a positive and accurate way in the Christian-dominated mainstream schools. Concern has also been expressed over the lack of attention given to the varied history, literature and culture of the Asian community and lack of encouragement for mother tongue languages. Some ethnic minority teachers also see separate schools as a means of avoiding the racism they have encountered in mainstream schools, which they feel has harmed their employment and promotion prospects. Many ethnic minority parents also see separate schools as a means of insulating their children from racist attitudes and behaviour. Some Muslim organisations have suggested these schools would offer a valuable means of fostering multi-racial understanding by enabling children to become secure in their cultural and religious roots. Such children would develop a confident and balanced view of their place in society free from a sense of alienation which is experienced by some of them.

Views recently put forward by Muslim organisations have also raised different issues relating specifically to adherence to Islamic religious and moral principles. Much of the evidence from Muslim groups was concerned with the religious 'rights and duties' of Muslim parents and children in an educational context, for example in relation to school uniform, school meals, physical education and religious instruction. Some Muslim groups have come to believe that mainstream schools cannot realistically be expected to accommodate Muslim requirements and that separate schools are necessary. The main role of Muslim schools is seen as educating children to be first and foremost 'good Muslims', and all other aspects of education are seen as of secondary concern. Religion would be taught in a 'confessional' style and amount to instruction designed to confirm children in their Islamic faith.

Within this debate the establishment of single-sex schools has become of primary concern for Muslim communities. It is the education of Muslim girls in the mainstream schools which has given most grounds for discontent. Many Muslim groups have called for separate schools for girls in which the curriculum would focus on education for marriage and motherhood in a particular Islamic sense, with other subjects receiving less attention and with the notion of careers education being seen as irrelevant to the pattern of adult life which girls were likely to pursue. The existing single-sex schools, within the mainstream, would not therefore be sufficient to satisfy many Muslims' requirements for their daughters' education. It is claimed that Islamic education for girls would in no sense be a 'second class' education, but would give them greater respect for and recognition of the specific role they can be expected to fulfil within their community.

The need, however, is for *all* pupils to share a common educational experience which prepares them for life in a truly pluralist society. To achieve this, *all* schools need to reappraise their curriculum provision and the attitudes which underlie their work, in order to challenge and overcome 'barriers' which at present exist between the majority and minority communities. If these changes do occur, particularly in relation to religious education, 'pastoral' concerns and language needs, then this will go a considerable way towards meeting the concerns of many ethnic minority parents, including those concerns which have led many to call for separate schools. If ethnic minority parents were able to exercise some direct influence over policy development and decision-making through governing bodies, this would also enhance their confidence in existing schools.

Creating an artificially separate situation in which children are taught exclusively by teachers from the same ethnic group is not desirable from the point of view of the children, the minority community or society as a whole. Separate schools cannot therefore be supported on these grounds. The only way of ensuring that minority communities are able both to retain their religious, cultural and linguistic heritages, and to be accorded full equality, is within the broader pluralist context for which the report argues. Separate schools could well fail to tackle many of the underlying concerns of the communities and might also exacerbate the very feelings of rejection which they were seeking to overcome. By, in effect, constituting a real and physical manifestation of the psychological barriers and divisions which exist in our society, they might well serve to reinforce and extend these rather than help to remove them. Separate schools would furthermore tend to absolve existing schools from the responsibility to reappraise and revise their practices. They would leave the educational and social experience of the remaining pupils impoverished.

Within the co-educational system, schools must do more to ensure that, where there is parental concern about girls participating in activities in a mixed group, there is a degree of single-sex provision in certain areas of the curriculum. It is clear, however, that such provision can go only some way towards allaying the concerns of those who desire a fully single-sex education for girls. The demise of mainstream single-sex schools over recent years has removed the option for many Muslim parents of having their daughters educated in what would be an acceptable environment. LEAs with multi-racial populations should think very carefully about the implications of declining single-sex provision in their areas for Muslim parents.

Of course, existing single-sex provision would not satisfy the demands of those Muslim parents who wish their daughters to have an Islamic education. But the kind of education which some Muslim groups have proposed cannot be supported. The principle of full equality of opportunity for boys and girls in terms of access to all aspects of the curriculum and equal rights, to be encouraged to think positively about one's place in the world, to be stretched intellectually, and to be equipped with the skills necessary to function as a full member of adult society, is fundamental to the philosophy of education in this country, and the notion of equal opportunity is enshrined in law. But far more must be done by schools to respond to the 'pastoral' needs of Muslim pupils so that parents can see that existing schools are prepared to respect their requirements and wishes.

As the law stands those communities who would still not be satisfied that their children's educational needs were being fully met would be entitled to establish their own voluntary-aided schools. If such schools are established, it is hoped that the misgivings about them will prove unfounded and that they will provide an education comparable to that offered elsewhere in the maintained system and would adequately prepare pupils for our multicultural society.

Some West Indian parents, too, have called for the establishment of separate schools, not on religious grounds but on the grounds that existing schools are irredeemably racist and can never provide black children with an understanding of, and pride in, their ethnic origins. Black children will never get a 'fair deal' unless schools are controlled by black people. This attitude has developed due to the fact that so many West Indians fail to fulfil their true potential and many parents feel that efforts by schools to remedy this are little more than tinkering and are of little value.

As with the establishment of separate schools on religious grounds, this would not offer a positive way forward for the ethnic minority communities or society as a whole. If the principles underlying 'Education for All' are acted upon, the main objectives of separate schools would be achieved within the mainstream system.

Six members of the Committee dissented from the view taken by the majority on the issue of 'separate schools'. They argued that it is unjust not to recommend positive assistance for their establishment, given the present state of affairs in mainstream schools, and given the fact that the principles of 'Education for All' are not yet accepted. An emphasis on an ideal future (when 'Education for All' is a reality) may be an excuse for inaction in the present, and for a failure to meet immediate needs. Furthermore, a number of separate schools would provide invaluable experience and evidence in the long journey towards the goal of 'Education for All' which all members of the Committee seek.

7. Teacher education and the employment of ethnic minority teachers

The policies advocated throughout the report clearly place particular responsibilities on the teaching profession, since teachers are the key figures in the education process.

Initial training

There appears to be confusion within teacher training institutions over two distinct forms of multicultural provision: on the one hand, provision designed to give student teachers the particular knowledge and skills needed to teach in a multi-racial *school* and, on the other hand, the preparation of all students for teaching in a multi-racial *society*, irrespective of whether the students concerned will be teaching in an 'all-white' or multi-racial school.

It has already been made clear that *all* schools have a responsibility to offer their pupils an education which reflects the realities of life in multi-racial Britain. *All* teachers must therefore be equipped to carry out this responsibility.

The training of teachers to teach in a multicultural context cannot be done in a 'mechanistic' way, involving merely adding a little here or taking away a little there, whilst leaving the main body of the students' educational experience untouched. On the contrary, a multicultural awareness must be developed by 'permeation', ie, all aspects of training courses must be permeated with the principles underlying a genuinely pluralist approach. All courses should recognise the diverse cultural context of which the sociology, psychology and philosophy of education should take account. Subject-specific courses should also be permeated with the pluralist perspective, for example, by discussing the development of scientific and mathematical concepts in different cultures, by broadening the range of literature, art and music drawn upon in subject studies, etc.

It is important to recognise, however, that permeation alone cannot be regarded as providing adequate preparation for teaching in a multi-racial society without additional specialist course work. By its very nature, it is difficult to measure the progress permeation has made in training institutions, but it seems clear that progress has not matched the rhetoric devoted publicly to the concept of permeation. Given this, there is a strong case in the immediate future for some reference to be made to pluralist issues within the central and compulsory 'core' of the initial training received by *all* teachers.

All 'core' courses should give students an informed awareness of the diversity of society. This would include basic 'facts and figures' about immigration and emigration, the circumstances which have conditioned the experiences and aspirations of different minority groups, and also the theory and practice of racism at institutional and individual level. Specialist optional courses relating to pluralist issues should continue to be offered as an opportunity for further in-depth study. Further, efforts should be made by all teacher training institutions to ensure that all their students have an opportunity to gain some practical experience in a multi-racial school.

The recently established Council for the Accreditation of Teacher Education (CATE) could have a vital role to play in accelerating the incorporation of a pluralist perspective in initial training courses. CATE has been asked to review all existing courses and to scrutinise proposals for new courses. One of the criteria to be used by CATE to evaluate courses includes the role of the course in developing an understanding of the type of society in which pupils are growing up, with its cultural and racial mix. The Secretary of State for Education should ask CATE to pay particular attention to the need to incorporate a pluralist perspective in all initial teacher training courses.

If a teacher has negative attitudes towards ethnic minorities and the development of a culturally plural society, then he or she will remain an inadequate teacher of *any* child in *any* school. If a student demonstrates, by his or her actions or behaviour during taught studies or teaching practice, deep-seated and openly racist views which materially affect the way he or she teaches and which do not appear to be open to reason or change through training, that should be an important element in assessing whether he or she is suitable to enter the teaching profession.

In-service training

Given the fact that the majority of teachers in schools today began their careers before the days of Commonwealth immigration and certainly before the emergence of the debate about the need for the education of *all* children to reflect a pluralist perspective, in-service training takes on added importance.

Induction training is designed to introduce newly qualified staff to a school, to prepare them for their specific responsibilities and offer them general advice and practical help and support. An HMI survey (*The New Teacher in School*, 1981) found that nearly half of the secondary teachers and just over three-fifths of the primary teachers appeared to be receiving satisfactory LEA support on entry to a new school. Over two-thirds of both primary and secondary schools were providing an environment which encouraged the professional development of new teachers. The HMI observed that 'the inadequacies of as many as one third of those (schools) in the sample may lead to the new teachers failing to achieve their potential – or at least in their doing so more painfully and more slowly'. There is an urgent need, therefore, for a major expansion in provision for induction training by both LEAs and schools.

A newly qualified or, equally, an experienced teacher entering a multi-racial school for the first time will need substantial induction training to provide him or her with the background knowledge needed to offer all pupils an appropriate and relevant education, free from stereotypes of particular minority groups, and to recognise the opportunities offered in a multi-racial situation.

All induction training in multi-racial areas should cover the following issues: how to avoid ethnocentrism within particular subjects; how to handle racism amongst pupils; how to relate to pupils from a wide range of backgrounds and experiences; how to meet the particular needs of some minority pupils, for example in terms of language; how to support and be sensitive to any cultural and religious factors which might influence their lives (but without stereotyping or placing undue emphasis on 'problems'); and how to utilise positively the range of pupils' experiences within schools.

Training provided for head teachers and senior staff by the National Development Centre for School Management Training in Bristol and other institutions should also ensure that a pluralist perspective is incorporated.

The coverage of multicultural issues within high level, award-bearing courses should be expanded in order to extend the capacity of the teacher training system to encourage the senior, key figures within the education service to an understanding of the implications, opportunities and responsibilities of teaching in a culturally diverse society so that they would be in a position to act as 'agents of change' within their own organisations and institutions.

Specialist short courses, although of limited value in themselves, can similarly be of considerable importance when viewed as part of a continuing in-service training and curriculum development process and should be expanded.

An increasing number of short in-service courses have included an element of Racism Awareness Training. The objective of RAT is in keeping with the need to acknowledge and challenge manifestations of racism at institutional and individual level. However, given that those who participate tend to be teachers who have already been 'converted' to the aims of multicultural education, their usefulness is uncertain. Short RAT courses which are concerned so explicitly and directly with the complex issue of racism may stand less chance of effectively influencing the attitudes and behaviour of a teacher who has not previously considered this aspect of his or her work than would a longer and more broadly based in-service course or school-based activities which set racism within a wider perspective. There is an urgent need for research into the various RAT programmes which have been devised so far and the DES should fund an independent evaluation of the content and effectiveness of such courses.

There is virtually no in-service provision currently available which seeks to cater for teachers in 'all-white' areas. There is urgent need to develop appropriate courses across the range of provision, from options in high level award-bearing courses to part-time short courses, designed specifically to enable teachers from 'all-white' schools to incorporate a pluralist perspective in their work. Such provision would include the bringing of an informed awareness of the diversity of contemporary Britain, the theory and practice of racism and how it can be challenged, the changing perceptions of 'ethnic minority' education and the view of 'Education for All', and the straightforward *educational* grounds for broadening the curriculum to incorporate multicultural perspectives. Within this context, it should be possible in some courses to deal with more specific issues which may be of particular relevance to teachers concerned with particular phases of education or particular subject specialisms, for example the question of enhancing the language skills and awareness of linguistic diversity of pupils in a 'mono-lingual' classroom (discussed in 5). The government is therefore urged to establish a series of 'pilot projects' involving teacher training institutions, LEAs and schools in 'all-white' areas, designed to develop and disseminate good practice in this field.

Financial constraints have in recent years led many LEAs to reduce the number of teachers they are prepared to release for in-service training and present courses are often under-subscribed. Therefore the proposed expansion of in-service provision must be matched by appropriate financial support to enable teachers and LEAs to take full advantage of the training opportunities available. The recently announced DES scheme of direct grants for in-service training should be extended to allow for grants in respect of courses relating to 'Education for All'.

School-based in-service support for teachers can make a contribution to the professional development of the individual teachers as well as play a part in the development of the policies and practices of the school as a whole. School-based activities can be seen as the only effective means of influencing those teachers who received their initial training many years ago but may be the least likely to attend out of school in-service courses. Particular attention should therefore be given to the development of such support for teachers in developing an enhanced awareness of the implications of cultural diversity for their work. In particular, efforts should be made to develop and extend the use of 'distance learning' techniques in relation to in-service training, especially in 'all-white' areas. This would include the use of taped and video-taped material which can both broaden the expertise available to a school and also widen the horizons of teachers. The Open University, for example, has already developed particularly good courses and programmes, and it is hoped these will be extended.

Even more potentially immediate in its impact on schools can be the expansion of schemes for staff exchanges both between schools with similar circumstances and also between schools with widely different characters, and the DES is urged to consider initiating a centrally-funded scheme to facilitate teacher exchanges.

Each school is recommended therefore to develop in consultation with the LEA and its advisors a scheme for the in-service education of its teachers. Such a scheme could form part of the policy statement on 'Education for All' which LEAs should require of each school.

It is clear that the task envisioned for teacher education at both initial and in-service level makes great demands on the teacher training institutions and on individual teacher trainers. It may well be necessary therefore for some teacher trainers to become involved in a process of reappraisal, reorientation and even retraining themselves. Given the contraction of the teacher training system in recent years, and the scarcity of newly recruited teacher trainers with recent experience in multi-racial schools, efforts should be made to develop closer links between schools and teacher training institutions, for example through the secondment of practising teachers to assist trainers. Further to this, HM Inspectorate should issue guidance on provision for 'training the trainers' in relation to the demands of today's multi-racial society.

Employment of ethnic minority teachers

It is clear that ethnic minority groups are disproportionately under-represented in the teaching profession. There is, however, no firm statistical basis for any discussion of the numbers of ethnic minority teachers and such estimates as have been made in recent years have been both limited in scope and definitionally imprecise. For example, the CRE in evidence was only able to estimate that 'there may be 800 or more teachers of West Indian origin and a rather larger number of Asian origin, but no precise figures are available'. The collection of statistical data on the ethnic origins of teachers and student teachers (as recommended in the interim report but as yet not carried out by the government) is an essential element in seeking to tackle the issues of the admission of minority students to training courses and the recruitment and career advancement of minority teachers.

The under-representation of minority teachers is a matter of great concern which merits urgent attention and positive action. There is no doubt that minority teachers face racial discrimination in seeking employment and gaining promotion. Ethnic minority teachers' organisations gave evidence that minority teachers were less likely to gain permanent positions and were often able only to work as 'supply' teachers. The absence of statistical data makes it difficult to establish the extent of discrimination but as the CRE observed: 'What is most apparent is the widespread sense of frustration and bitterness among ethnic minority teachers about what they see as their subordinate and disadvantaged position in the teaching profession.'

Many minority teachers are 'stagnating' in the system, in posts far below both their capabilities and experience. Many have become discouraged and disenchanted with the obstacles which they felt had been placed in the way of their progress, and have left the profession. The CRE, and all those involved within LEAs and schools in making appointments, are urged to devote far greater efforts to identifying and overcoming racism within the teaching profession. All LEAs are urged to establish themselves as 'equal opportunity employers' and publicly adopt 'equal opportunity' policies.

Increasing the number of ethnic minority teachers is important for the following reasons:

- so that the staff of the education service (as in all areas of employment) are seen as a natural reflection of the make-up of the population;
- people from ethnic minorities should have opportunities to become professional workers if they have the desire and ability to do so;
- ethnic minority teachers act as a source of cultural expertise and skill for other staff and children;
- ethnic minority parents and children who are unable or unwilling to trust 'authority' to understand their needs are reassured by the presence of staff from their own ethnic group;
- ethnic minority teachers can serve as valuable 'role models' for pupils of the same ethnic background, who can see the teacher as someone who has faced and overcome the same hurdles they face.

Any type of 'quota' system to increase minority recruitment is, however, opposed as this would be likely to involve a diminution of standards. However, far more consideration should be given in making appointments to the extent to which a particular ethnic, cultural, linguistic or religious background is an additional and desirable feature for a job in any school.

The DES is asked to clarify the arrangements for granting qualified teacher status to minority teachers who possess overseas qualifications with a view to encouraging them to enter the teaching profession, as long as this involves no diminution of standards. (Concern has been expressed that the procedure is at present expensive and time-consuming for prospective teachers.)

Since 1977 'special access' courses have been established in seven LEAs to enable mature students (predominantly from ethnic minorities) who lacked the normal academic qualifications to undertake teacher training. It is hoped that there will be an expansion of access-style provision to the whole range of higher education in the future. The performance of students on special access courses should also be monitored, examining the experience of those who actually obtain teaching posts. Students on such courses are at present only eligible for discretionary awards. These must be made mandatory.

It is clear that the climate of racism in this country must be tackled to change the attitudes of minority pupils, few of whom at present aspire to a career in teaching. Specifically, careers teachers and officers, with the strong support of the DES and HMI, must positively encourage minority pupils to become teachers and to emphasise that they can aspire to playing an integral role within the teaching profession as a whole. The main obstacle to increased recruitment is still, however, their failure to gain the necessary academic qualifications. This adds further weight to the policies advocated to combat under-achievement.

8. 'Other' ethnic minority groups

The situation of children from some of the smaller ethnic minority communities has received rather less attention than Asian and West Indian groups. Attention was focused on some of these groups, either because they were seen as exemplars of particular types of communities, or because their needs were considered to be particularly deserving of attention in their own right. As the main findings and conclusions relating to the needs of ethnic minority children and to the development of 'Education for All' are contained elsewhere, the following section is confined to a discussion of their *particular* educational needs.

The educational needs of children of Chinese origin

A major issue in relation to the education of Chinese children is the difficulties many experience learning English. This is exacerbated by the dispersed nature of Chinese settlement, whereby many children are in schools which have little experience of ethnic minority children and no access to ESL support. A reluctance to complain may mean language problems remain unrecognised.

LEAs are encouraged to build up appropriate resources, including video tapes from language centres and peripatetic ESL teachers dealing with Chinese children, to improve language teaching provision. Resources should also be built up to enable teachers to impart an awareness of Chinese culture to all pupils.

There is no doubt that Chinese children and parents clearly appreciate teachers using elements of their cultural background in teaching since they see this as properly enhancing their culture in the eyes of the rest of the community. Many teachers did not realise how ignorant they were of other cultures. The lack of knowledge about Hong Kong and its economic importance to Britain was felt to be deplorable. Usually all that schools offered were token examples of Chinese festivals or cookery rather than introducing elements of Chinese history and geography into the curriculum and, where the number of pupils justified this, the teaching of the Chinese language for both Chinese and non-Chinese pupils.

Teachers should be wary of accepting their overall perception of Chinese pupils as being hard workers and high achievers, as they may well underestimate or overlook educational difficulties. The stereotype of high achiever is as dangerous as that of the low achiever and strengthens the view put forward of the need to regard all pupils on their own merits as individuals with differing needs and problems.

The dispersed nature of Chinese settlement serves to emphasise further the general conclusion that schools in predominantly all-white areas also need to adopt the broader 'Education for All' approach. The importance of the Chinese language in maintaining the community's identity was demonstrated by the firm commitment to community-based language classes.

The educational needs of children of Cypriot origin

There is a strong feeling amongst Greek and Turkish Cypriot parents that education is the responsibility of the teacher and that parents should not interfere. This is combined with a high degree of respect for the teacher's position which can make it a daunting prospect for parents who are not fluent in English to approach the school for advice or to discuss their children's progress. Many Cypriot parents who gave evidence were concerned with school discipline and behaviour, and some felt there was insufficient supervision of girls' 'conduct'. Many Turkish Cypriot parents felt the informality and flexibility of primary education in this country has not been sufficiently explained to parents.

None of the Turkish Cypriot representatives felt that many Turkish Cypriot parents would have much sympathy for the way some fundamentalist Muslim groups interpreted the 'rights and duties' of Muslim parents as regards religious observance. They also unanimously rejected the idea of Muslim voluntary aided schools, but were highly critical of the 'narrowness' of the religious education curriculum in many schools. Both Greek and Turkish Cypriot parents were strongly in favour of retaining the option of single-sex schools for girls.

Many parents were concerned with what they saw as inadequate ongoing ESL provision, and the risk that their children, while receiving tuition in basic 'survival' English, might subsequently be classified as 'slow learners'. There was a clear feeling that teachers saw 'lack of English' as a sign of 'lack of ability'. Much evidence was also received about the negative view many mainstream teachers take of second language learners.

Cypriot representatives strongly favoured both 'mother tongue maintenance' and 'mother tongue teaching' in mainstream schools: they were opposed to the withdrawal of pupils for ESL teaching. There are estimated to be approximately 50 language schools catering for the Greek Cypriot community in London, and 10-15 for the Turkish Cypriot community. Parents seemed, however, to want some language provision to be made during school hours.

Some Cypriot teachers stressed the great difficulties they felt they faced in gaining promotion and reaching positions of responsibility within schools. They referred to what they saw as the 'appalling' absence of any realistic coverage of multicultural concerns in their courses and also the hostile atmosphere they had encountered in staffrooms.

The 1980 ILEA Literacy Survey showed that Turkish Cypriot pupils had the lowest average reading attainment levels of all ethnic minority groups. While Greek Cypriot literacy levels were generally higher, by the age of eight they too had fallen below the scores of West Indians and were only higher than Turkish Cypriots.

Possible reasons given in evidence to explain the greater underachievement of Turkish Cypriots compared with Greek Cypriots included the following:

• since the Greek Cypriot community outnumbered the Turkish Cypriot community four to one, the former was seen as a more 'self-confident' community;

• the Greek Cypriot community had generally been better educated and more urbanised in Cyprus, compared with the rural-oriented Turkish Cypriots. (This explanation was *very strongly* refuted by some representatives of both communities, as presenting an entirely inaccurate picture.);

• the greater financial prosperity of the Greek Cypriots placed them in a better position to support their children's education;

• Greek Cypriots were more likely to 'pass for white' and were therefore less likely to be subject to racism;

• stereotyped views of the 'Turks' and 'Greeks' are very different: the Greeks were generally regarded and presented as the 'great civilisers of the world' and as being 'western', while the Turks were generally seen as uncivilised and cruel eastern 'barbarians', who had threatened civilisation, and were also adherents to a strange 'foreign' faith: Islam. These stereotypes were felt to have had a direct bearing on teachers' expectations of Turkish Cypriots. This argument, put forward by many in both the Turkish and Greek Cypriot communities, certainly constitutes a powerful argument for the wide-ranging and insidious influence of stereotyping on the experience of different ethnic minority groups.

The educational needs of children of Italian origin

The two major educational issues in relation to Italian children are language-related: the teaching of English as a second language, and arrangements for the maintenance and teaching of the 'mother tongue'.

It is apparent that there is considerable need amongst Italian children, including those born in Britain, for help and support with mastering English. Even where they might appear fluent, this might well mask more complex 'second stage' ESL needs. The 'invisibility' of Italian children, and the fact that they are often not regarded as an ethnic minority, might lead teachers to fail to recognise the possible difficulties which they might face. Several teachers referred to Italian children who had done well at infant level but who, at primary and secondary level, where they were called upon to apply their knowledge of English to increasingly complex and abstract concepts, had tended to fall behind and who had ultimately found themselves in remedial streams.

Unlike other ethnic minority languages, Italian has long been offered as a modern language. But some concern was expressed about the appropriateness of existing 'O' and 'A' level examinations in Italian for 'mother tongue' speakers of the language since it was felt that they called for an unnecessarily high level of English, rather than concentrating on the pupil's knowledge of Italian.

A unique factor with the Italian community is the extent to which the 'home' government offers direct support for the teaching of Italian in this country. The classes are organised on a regional basis and currently involve 1,500 teachers, recruited in Italy and employed by the Italian authorities. Classes can take place after school, on Saturdays or as part of the school day, when pupils are withdrawn from mainstream classes.

Italian teachers gave evidence that, because they were peripatetic, they often felt isolated from the rest of the pupils' school life. Much depended on attitudes of individual heads and staff. The teachers felt strongly that Italian should be taught during the school day, when pupils were generally more enthusiastic and 'mentally prepared'. They also felt that ESL needs should be met in mainstream classes.

The educational needs of children of Ukrainian origin

Ukrainian children now appear to be achieving well at school despite still being seen rather as 'oddities' by the host community. It also appears that proportionately more Ukrainian children go on to higher education and subsequently do well in the job market. However, Ukrainian community representatives expressed concern that 'the educational environment is not conducive to the development of the children's Ukrainian identity'. They were specifically concerned about the teaching of English, and the teachers' generally 'appalling ignorance' of Ukrainian children's cultural and home background.

The tendency for many teachers to confuse Ukrainian culture with Russian or Polish culture was especially offensive. Similarly the failure of teachers to try to pronounce Ukrainian names correctly was often referred to. It was felt that teacher training courses should make teachers much more aware of the importance of these matters and the positive role teachers should be playing in fostering the child's ethnic identity rather than denigrating it.

Concern was expressed about the practice of teaching ESL by withdrawing pupils from normal classes as it was felt this would hinder rather than aid their overall progress.

The Ukrainian community has a well-developed system of language and culture classes. Ukrainian may be taken at 'O' level at present and representatives were anxious to see it extended to 'A' level. The community would also welcome some grant support from LEAs towards the running of language classes and more cooperation between mainstream and community-based teachers.

The educational needs of Vietnamese children

The major issue for Vietnamese youngsters is the acquisition of English, especially for those arriving in the upper secondary age range for whom provision for ESL support may be very limited.

The official policy of dispersing the Vietnamese refugees around the country, especially to areas which had had little previous experience of catering for children for whom English was a second language, had clearly made the task of teaching English considerably harder. Initiatives were further hampered by the fact that expenditure on provision for the Vietnamese is not covered by section 11 grants. The dispersal policy, although it may have been based on good intentions, is in fact an example of institutional racism given the underlying assumption that large groups of Vietnamese in one area would inevitably cause resentment.

Vietnamese parents, as with many other minority groups, tended to leave their children's education largely to teachers. While parents always wished their children to succeed, they often had only a vague idea of what this would entail, in terms of examinations, etc. As with Chinese children, the teachers' general impression that Vietnamese children were highly motivated might be concealing both language problems and problems caused by the 'refugee trauma' – especially severe in the Vietnamese case.

It is apparent that much of the initial goodwill generated in Britain by the plight of the 'boat people' has now evaporated and been replaced by resentment and racism.

The educational needs of 'Liverpool Blacks'

'Liverpool Blacks' have been included as a separate group firstly because they have fared worse than any other group, with the exception of travellers, in educational and career achievements, and secondly (and paradoxically) because this group appears to be more closely assimilated with the 'majority' by ancestry, language, culture and length of residence than any other group. Its continued academic underachievement therefore shows the fallacy of expecting educational underachievement to disappear automatically as language and cultural differences are overcome.

The term 'Liverpool Black' describes the black community established in Liverpool since the 19th century of African, African/English and some Asian descent. They are totally 'assimilated' with the white community in terms of language and culture, but just as totally excluded from the majority community's employment and social environment.

There is ample evidence that black and white Liverpudlian children are dramatically underachieving due to low staff morale, lack of resources, and the alienation amongst pupils and parents in the midst of a general atmosphere of city decline. For example, an HMI Report (*Educational Provision by Liverpool Education Authority in the Toxteth Area*, 1982) found that in one comprehensive school in Toxteth only 30 per cent of the intake had a reading age of 10 or more on entry. However, it is clear that 'Liverpool Blacks' are underachieving to an even greater extent, partly because of the negative attitude towards them of some teachers, and partly because of their own and their parents' sense of alienation in a social structure that offers them no hope for the future. During a visit to Liverpool evidence was heard of only two 'Liverpool Blacks' who had gone to university. There were no 'Liverpool Blacks' at Liverpool University.

The most important lesson to be learnt from the experience of 'Liverpool Blacks' is that racial disadvantage in this case is in no way the result of cultural problems of 'newness', or language problems. In this area, where an ethnic minority suffers racial disadvantage to a greater extent than anywhere else in Britain, it is purely the result of racism.

The educational needs of travellers' children

Due to the shortage of official camp sites, nearly half of all travellers are forced to lead an unstable and unsettled existence on illegal encampments. The problem therefore of parents not feeling they can risk sending their children to school *at all* (when their caravans may be moved on at any time of the day) is a major one. The Plowden Report claimed that less than 10 per cent of travellers' children attended school at all.

However, even traveller parents living securely on an official site may be reluctant to send their children to school. In the eyes of many, education is seen solely in terms of literacy and numeracy, and the broader concept of education, especially at secondary level, is seen as irrelevant and unnecessary. Others may reject the education system of a society which has so clearly rejected them. Some parents are fearful that their children's presence in school may confirm in others prejudicial cultural stereotypes. Academic backwardness, as a result of a previous lack of schooling, and unusual behaviour are thought by many parents to be images that would be interpreted in negative terms by schools.

The 1980 Education Act unequivocally places a duty on LEAs to ensure that appropriate full-time education is provided for all children residing in their area, whether permanently or temporarily, and regardless of the legal status of the camp site where they live. Many traveller organisations believe some LEAs are failing to fulfil these responsibilities and that traveller children are being intentionally deprived of their right to education.

In many ways, the situation of travellers' children throws into stark relief many of the factors which influence the education of children from other ethnic minority groups – racism, myths, stereotypes, the inappropriateness and inflexibility of the education system, and the need for better links between homes and schools and teachers and parents. Many of the official attitudes to travelling families tend towards encouraging them to 'settle down' and in effect to cease being travellers. Within the overall philosophy of 'Education for All' ways can and must be found to reconcile the concerns and aspirations of the travelling community and the mainstream education system in a much more positive manner.

Additional educational support should be provided within the mainstream system, although some children may require some form of 'bridge' into normal schools. Only for the small minority of children from families which are almost continually on the move should any form of provision on-site be considered in any way desirable. Each LEA should have a 'named person' to coordinate work in the field of traveller education.

Appendix: annexes to the report

Racism: theory and practice

The Role of the Media: a background paper by Dr G K Verma
Multi-ethnic Teaching and the Pupils: self-concepts: a paper by Peter A Green

Achievement and underachievement

Achievement and Underachievement: Evidence from Young People of Afro-Caribbean and Asian Origin
Results from the School Leavers Survey 1981/82: a paper by DES Statistics Branch
The Education of Bangladeshi Children in Tower Hamlets: A Background Paper by the Education Office, Inner London Education Authority
The IQ Question: a paper by Professor N J Mackintosh and Dr C G N Mascie-Taylor
Revised Research Proposal on 'Academically Successful Black Pupils', submitted by the Research and Statistics Branch of the Inner London Education Authority
Summary of Main Findings of a Longitudinal Study by Dr G K Verma
A Note on Research: a paper by Mr J Cornford

Multicultural education: further studies

Extracts from Professor John Rex's Introduction to the Report on the Development of Multicultural Education Policy in Four Local Education Authority Areas
'All White' Schools Project: Outline
A Report of Visits to Schools with Few or No Ethnic Minority Pupils by Arnold Matthews
A Report of Visits to Schools with Few or No Ethnic Minority Pupils by Laurie Fallows

'Education for all: a new approach'

'Education for Racial Equality': policy document from Berkshire LEA
Examples of Anti-Racist Statements adopted by Two Multi-Racial Secondary Schools

Language and language education

Extract from evidence submitted by a multi-racial secondary school we visited describing their approach to co-operative teaching
Extracts from evidence submitted to us by a head of English and an ESL teacher describing how their school moved from ESL teaching on a withdrawal basis to provision within the mainstream curriculum
RSA Diploma in the Teaching of English as a Second Language in Multicultural Schools: Syllabus (Autumn 1983)
Extracts from Linguistic Minorities in England: A Report from the Linguistic Minorities Project (LMP) – July 1983
EC Directive on Education of Children of Migrant Workers
Training of Teachers of Ethnic Minority Community Languages – a summary of a research project conducted by Professor M Craft and Dr M Atkins of the University of Nottingham
West Indian Language: implications of the repertoire position for practice
Extract from *Modern Languages in the Curriculum* by Professor Eric Hawkins
Extracts from *The Languages Book*, ILEA 1981

Religion and the role of the school

Extracts from the Education Act 1944

Extract from Religious Heritage and Personal Quest — Guidelines for Religious Education — Berkshire LEA 1982

Extract from evidence from a Primary School setting out its aims of Religious Education and describing a number of projects which had been undertaken

Extracts from evidence submitted by Multi-Racial Secondary Schools setting out their aims and objectives of Religious Education

The Establishment of Voluntary Aided Schools — Background Explanatory Notes by the DES

Teacher education and the employment of ethnic minority teachers

Paper by Derek Cherrington and Ray Giles summarising the Findings of the National Survey of Multicultural Aspects of Teacher Training

Paper by HMI Ivor Ambrose summarising the Findings of an Inspection Exercise to Investigate the Coverage of Multicultural Education in Initial and In-Service Teacher Training Courses

Extracts from Evidence received from Two Teacher Training Institutions reflecting the underlying principles of Permeation

Extracts from Evidence illustrating the ways in which Multicultural Issues have been incorporated in the Core Studies of various Teacher Training Institutions

Extracts from Evidence relating to Optional Courses offered by various Teacher Training Institutions

Extracts from Evidence describing the work undertaken in a PGCE Option Course in Multicultural Education at a University Department of Education

Council for National Academic Awards — Multicultural Education: Discussion Paper

Data from Little and Willey's Research Report 'Studies in the Multi-Ethnic Curriculum' relating to In-Service Training.

National Programme of 'Training the Trainers' Courses

Admissions of Ethnic Minorities to Teacher Education Studies from Access Courses

The educational needs of children of Chinese origin

Extracts from *Community Education: The Unknown Perspective — Chinese Mother Tongue Classes* by Ming Tsow

The educational needs of children of Italian origin

Outline of the EC Sponsored Project 'Mother Tongue and Culture in Bedfordshire'

The educational needs of Vietnamese children

Language — an Extract from 'Vietnamese Children in Derby'

Article taken from *The Times* 12 March 1983

The educational needs of travellers' children

Extracts from *The Education of Travellers' Children*, HMI Discussion Document. DES, 1983

The Runnymede Trust

The Runnymede Trust is a registered educational charity set up in 1968. Its objectives are the collection and dissemination of information and the promotion of public education on immigration and race relations. This is done in a number of ways:

- An information service which provides information on race and immigration.
- A reference library of books, pamphlets and press cuttings which may be used by prior appointment.
- A monthly bulletin, *Race and Immigration.*
- Publication of pamphlets and papers on matters of current interest and concern.
- Seminars and meetings.

A full list of publications and details of subscriptions to *Race and Immigration* are available on request.

Runnymede Trust
37A Grays Inn Road
London WC1X 8PP
01-404 5266

Other publications of interest

Racism and Discrimination in Britain: a select bibliography 1970-83
Paul Gordon and Francesca Klug
£3.50 (+30p p&p)

Different Worlds: racism and discrimination in Britain
Paul Gordon and Francesca Klug
An illustrated pamphlet suitable for use in secondary schools
£1.00 (inc p&p)

British Immigration Control: a brief guide
Paul Gordon and Francesca Klug
An illustrated account of the history and working of immigration control
£1.00 (+25p p&p)

Advisory Approaches to Multicultural Education
Arnold Matthews
Surveys the organisational framework and policies of local advisors
£1.50 (+30p p&p)

Race and Immigration: the Runnymede Trust bulletin
Monthly bulletin covering all aspects of race relations and immigration in Britain
£10 pa (institutions), £8 pa (voluntary bodies), £6 pa (individuals)

Available from the Runnymede Trust, 37A Grays Inn Road, London WC1X 8PP